Your Life as It Is

YOUR LIFE AS IT IS

by

A. Molotkov

Accents Publishing • Lexington, Kentucky • 2014

Copyright © 2014 by A. Molotkov
All rights reserved

Printed in the United States of America

Accents Publishing
Editor: Katerina Stoykova-Klemer
Cover Image: Anatoly Molotkov
Cover Design: Simeon Kondev

ISBN: 978-1-936628-29-2
First Edition

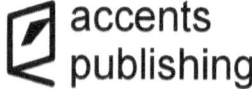

Accents Publishing is an independent press for brilliant voices. For a catalog of current and upcoming titles, please visit us on the Web at

www.accents-publishing.com

for Laurie,
written on a shared trip to Russia in May 2011

You wake up in the morning.
You go outside.
This is your life as it is.

You wake up in the morning and get out of bed. The carnival is in town. The signs are unmistakable. The calliope song. The smells. The excited voices.

Your husband is making breakfast. He is humming something to himself. You would rather have silence, but you will not say anything.

> Your last year's footprint is this year's mudslide. The pawns are running an election to select the king. You receive your own radio transmission from the future. It is encrypted, you don't know the cipher yet.

You go outside. The bright red sunset is the same as the last time. Perhaps it's the same day. Perhaps it's the same you. Possibly, it's the same world.

You wake up in the morning. A blind woman is standing over your bed, her face impassive, her hands folded on her chest. She is wearing a blue dress, the kind of blue only a repressed human being could invent.

Instead of saying anything, you just keep staring. You know she knows you are no longer asleep. Your wife is using her sewing machine: the tender percussion of racing stitches.

> Your former future has become your recent past. Promises should be taken as good intentions: that's the only way to play it safe. The king is no longer interested in being the center of attention. You emit signals that only those who don't care about you will notice.

You go outside. You want to ask the blind woman what she is doing here, but when you open your mouth, she is gone. You must be asleep, but she is convinced that you are not.

You wake up in the morning. Nothing is out of the ordinary. You count to one hundred. This is the time you allow yourself before you get out of bed and start your boring day.

Your dog runs in with a toy in his mouth. He wants to play. But you have too much to do. You pet him absentmindedly. The hair on his muzzle is grey, just like you remember it.

> Your interaction with yourself adopts the form of a monologue. You often refer to yourself as he. You refer to others too infrequently. The king walks off the board, indifferent to the battle other pieces wage. The radio transmission disclosed that something was missing, and now you know what it is. You are a blind person.

You go outside. It is raining. It has been raining for days. The rain is the sound it makes, your wet hair. You try to imagine what it might look like, but you have no frame of reference. Nothing you imagine has sight.

You wake up in the morning. There will come an age when the fact of a new awakening is a gift in and of itself. But you are blissfully far from that point. You wonder if the carnival is in town—you listen for the familiar sounds, but they are missing. It must not be the time yet. Then you remember about your hearing loss.

Your brother has not written for a month or two. You are going through your recent interactions to determine if you may have inadvertently offended him. People always arrive at wrong conclusions.

> Your past is like a street light at midnight. Your wishes evolve into acceptance. The queen is unhappy that the king is getting all the attention, but she wouldn't want to be in his shoes. Your successes may be indicative of your failure to relax.

You go outside. The blind woman is nowhere to be seen. You are relieved that you don't have to encounter her today. She may have fallen asleep.

You wake up in the morning. Getting out of bed is the last thing you want to do. It is snowing, the trees are beautiful and indifferent, their white foliage immaterial like your life.

You hear a child's voice, half-singing half-mumbling indistinctly. For a moment, you can't remember if it's your own child, whether it's a boy or a girl. You may still be asleep. You wonder if you should get up and dive into your life. Perhaps you have more time to linger.

> Your past is your present turned inside out. There is nothing awaiting you that you have not already imagined. A factual achievement may not be superior to an imaginary one. The bishop is annoyed with having to move diagonally. He longs for the white fields, so close and so inaccessible. An intense, passionate existence is not necessarily a good recipe for a superior afterlife.

You go outside. The snow is gone, the trees have turned green. Perhaps you were looking out the wrong window. The child's voice you heard just a minute ago disappears. The child must have grown up. Next, your house disappears. You too may have reached adulthood. You keep walking.

You wake up in the morning and find yourself in the middle of a snow-covered field. Miniscule on the horizon stands an outline of the place you call home. The only path you can see leads away from it.

Your husband is walking toward you across the vast distance. His figure is tiny, but his enormous shining eyes are like moons over the spare landscape.

> Somewhere along the way your smile turned into a grimace. You have tried to mark your every turn so you can make your way out of the labyrinth. But the paint has run out. Knights and bishops are laughing at you from a nearby hill. Then you notice that the walls are two feet high. If you hadn't looked down all your life, you would have realized this sooner.

You go outside. The street is brightly decorated. Cheerful balloons of all colors are tied to benches, street signs, even the parked cars. But there is no one in sight. It is conceivable that the whole world exists exclusively for your sake.

You wake up in the morning. The carnival sounds you heard just a minute ago belong to your dream. The waking life is the same as the dream, but without the carnival. You have to warm up your car.

Your wife was supposed to make the tea, but the thermos is empty. You get upset, but when you check on her, her body is rounded onto itself. You touch her forehead. It's cold and impenetrable like other dreams that have slipped away. You don't have to close her eyes.

> Your handwriting had turned illegible before arriving on the paper. This is the nature of your thoughts. A black and white couple of pawns get married and improvise a new game.

You go outside. The little girl rides her bicycle by your front porch. The wheels are frozen, as if she is in a film. You realize you too may be in a film. You look around for a camera, but your own eyes are the camera and the source of light.

You wake up in the morning and find yourself floating in the middle of an ocean. You should be worried, but strangely enough, you are not. You know there must exist a current that will take you home.

Your daughter did not do her homework, and now everything may be lost. She was sent home without lunch and without the right to a bright future. You suspect that your own punishment is even more severe.

> The mysteries you were puzzling over have not been solved, but they have become irrelevant. The queen underwent transgender surgery, rendering your pieces defenseless against your opponent. You have forgotten who your opponent is.

You go outside. The sun is bright. The blind woman is at the street corner. She looks as if she is waiting for you. Her expression makes you uneasy—you know she is aware of your presence. "Where are you going?" she asks. You wish you knew.

You wake up in the morning. The silence of the world around you puzzles you. The birds, the cars and the ocean all decided to take a break at the same time. Then you remember about your recent hearing loss. The sounds you heard in your dreams were transmissions from the past.

Your wife is drifting on a block of ice, carried by the fast current of a black river. She is waving to you in horror, only a few solid inches around her separating her from a cold, liquid death. You are running down the riverbank, trying to keep up. You know you must do something to save her, but you are not sure what. You stop to tie your shoes.

> Your plans have become memories of plans. You missed the moment when this transition took place. Recently you had a way out of this predicament. You shared your escape strategy with a rook, and now every pawn knows all about it, even though you have forgotten.

You go outside. The simple truths of air, trees, sky, ground are no longer satisfactory, nor undeniable. You find yourself floating over the earth, your body horizontal. You can see both the sky and the land without turning around.

You wake up in the morning. The blind man is sitting on the edge of your bed, swaying in rhythm to the sounds of a song only he can hear. It's odd to see tears streaming down from his eyes. You did not expect faulty eyes to retain some of their functionality.

Your wife walks in and addresses you, but you don't register her words. You must still be half-asleep. You are surprised that she pays the blind man absolutely no attention, as if his presence here were not unexpected.

> Your yesterday's song has become today's avalanche. The roaring waves of snow eliminate all obstacles in your path. You think about it for a moment and realize that it is, in fact, someone else's path. The pawns glare at you in condemnation before being swept away.

You go outside. The tranquility of this summer morning reminds you that life is essentially peaceful. All you have to do is to lean into it, let it carry you along. But you have become too heavy from the sadness and the pessimism that stick to you as you advance through time.

You wake up in the morning. You are happy to see another day unfolding before you. There is much to do and see. You had plans for today, but at the moment, all of them seem utterly unimportant. You decide to improvise.

Your son is humming a tune in the next room, something vague under his breath. The melody is familiar, but hard as you try, you can't place it. When you enter the room, it's empty. You remember what happened to your son.

> The king is mad about having to spend the entire game undercover. You did not play it safe. You made a mistake of wanting too much from the world. Your friends are happy with their enjoyable, less demanding lives. You don't have any friends.

You go outside. The carnival crew are packing. There is more emotional energy in an ending than a beginning. All endings are preconceived. The birds sound as if they disagree with this simple fact.

You wake up in the morning without a frame of reference. People always arrive at wrong conclusions. Since your dog died, you find your monologues empty, as if every statement you make has already been uttered by someone else, in a more appropriate context.

You remember last time you traveled abroad. The buzzing crowds whose language you could not understand intimidated you. You have remained in your own town ever since, unwilling to give up your familiar comforts. Your wife has to travel with a friend.

> When you listen carefully, the words you will say during your remaining days can be heard as soft, hesitant whispers. If you could understand them, you would learn how to avoid the pitfalls that are otherwise inescapable. You know you will have to wait for that knowledge to arrive too late. The king and the queen are in bed, laughing at you.

You go outside. The house you have always lived in has been replaced by another building. You wonder whether you will be able to reenter your life by going back inside, but you are too afraid to try it. The bells of a missing church resound nearby.

You wake up in the morning. A boom microphone is placed over your bed, and in the window, a poorly concealed camera muzzle can be seen. You wonder if you are in a film.

Perhaps there is a better way—one you have not thought of. The best answers to your questions always come to others. Your silence is not your own. Your family, real and imaginary, own all the answers.

> Your blind eyes hunger for visual information. A hope that one day you might miraculously regain your sight has never quite left you, despite the utter absurdity of such a hope. You have heard that truly inexplicable things are likely to happen at a moment's notice. The knights suffer from neck pain caused by the crooked moves they are forced to make.

You go outside and find yourself on a rapidly moving train. A little boy peeks at you from the seat ahead. When you smile to him, he flashes a return smile and hides his face. Life is a series of curious glances, exploratory words, shy smiles.

You wake up in the morning. A strange sound penetrates your room. You have to focus to understand what it is. A child, crying. You must have done something to cause the child's unhappiness. You try to remember if you have a child of your own. You wonder why it is so easy to assume guilt.

Your husband is using his power tools in the shed, and you realize you are completely uninterested in his current endeavor. This is what it means to love someone for a long time.

> Your memory is like a fake fairy tale, reenacted. The queen smiles and takes off her clothes. Then she takes off her skin, and finally her flesh. Her skeleton is both a question mark and an exclamation point.

You go outside. The snow has melted before falling again. The world looks as if nothing had changed. This is what happens when changes replace changes. You close your eyes.

You wake up in the morning. The mysteries of your life are encoded with a cipher that is vaguely familiar, yet the precise clue eludes you. It would help if you could understand more about it, but as things stand, you seem to understand less and less.

The child that was crying earlier has quieted down. Unexpectedly, the silence is unsettling. You worry that something tragic may have happened. Something tragic always happens, but most of the time these events take place elsewhere.

> The sounds that you can no longer hear cut through to you through your deafness. The images of things you can no longer see have taken up permanent residence in your mind. You have heard and seen enough. The king and the queen are dancing a slow dance in your memory. You often refer to yourself as she and forget about others.

You go outside. The snow has been falling all night, and now the path to the gate is completely covered. There may be no gate, and most likely, there is no house. You are naked. You must invent another way to survive.

You wake up in the morning. The world feels strange in some intangible way. You lie with your eyes closed, trying to determine what is causing this impression. The universe may be different, but on the other hand, the difference may be wholly within you.

Your mother used to look at you disapprovingly. Since her death, you have no way to determine whether her criticism was real or imaginary. You wish you could ask her several simple questions that are always on the tip of your tongue.

> A pawn is conspiring to make it all the way across the board, causing a conflict of interest in the queen's mind. The king has fallen asleep. The radio transmission you are trying to send is not properly encoded. You must seek help if you want it to make sense upon reception.

You go outside. You feel you may be forgetting something important. The vast green field is swaying in the wind, unaware of the fact that it is a black and white photograph taken in winter.

You wake up in the morning. The little boy is standing by your bed with a question on his lips, but he is numb, and you can't read lips. You need an interpreter, but the world eludes interpretation.

Your sister is lost in a vast field covered with snow. You decide to go out and try to rescue her, but your feet become the tip of a pencil and the field, a sheet of paper. You realize you must write something significant, but to do so, you must learn words. Your handwriting alone might not suffice.

> Your opponent has been making much progress, but it's not an issue: you have resigned yourself to a life without a bright future. You suspect you may be a pawn, but there is something heavy mounted on your head. Your smiles have become deflated from exposure. Tomorrow you will need to be yourself, perhaps for the first time.

You go outside. The blind man is aiming a gun at you, and you know that your chances of escaping are immaterial like a kiss from an affair you had when you were young. Now the world itself is young, but you have become old.

You wake up in the morning and open your eyes. Your room is crowded. Your old friends, long dead, have come to honor you. Their eyes are kind, as if they had forgiven you all the offenses you unwittingly committed.

Your husband is holding on to a tree branch suspended over a deep canyon. You are standing on the edge, wishing to help him, but as much as you try, you can't reach him. In panic, you scan the area for something you could use to help him hold his weight. There is nothing but pine cones and dry leaves. You bend over to tie your shoes.

> The king and the queen have retired. They took up residence off the board. You can see their house from your front porch. The smoke from their barbeque causes you to tear up in fake grief.

You go outside. The heavy orange sky is oppressive like a dying love affair. The day must be ending. You missed its beginning. You missed many things you would have loved. Perhaps missed people and opportunities is what life is all about.

You wake up in the morning. The clouds outside your window are strangely immobile, as if they were painted on the glass. Perhaps the wind is still asleep. You realize it would be nice to do something meaningful today, but no specific ideas come to mind.

Your husband's car is still in the driveway. You are surprised he has not left for work. It's not like him. You walk out into the living room and find him resting on your beautiful hardwood floor. You don't feel anything at the thought of his absence.

> Your skin is a reflection of your attempts to get closer to the true meaning of your life, but you suspect that it might be inside out. The bishop has given up faith and no longer finds satisfaction in diagonal existence. You remember your own memories better than your past.

You walk outside and find yourself on another street, next to another house. You might have been a different person all along, or perhaps there is a better explanation for all of this.

You wake up in the morning. You are in the middle of a vast empty square, sharp nails of skyscrapers piercing the clouds on all sides. You must be here for a meeting, but you can't remember with whom. The buildings are identical.

Your dead mother is surprised to see you. Her lips move, but no sound is produced. You realize that you have gone deaf. You try to read her lips, but they don't appear to be forming words. You take her by the hand to guide her out of this place. Her hand is small.

> The smile on the king's face is guarded, as if he were trying to encourage you without offering any concrete guarantees. The ambulance arrives to pick up the pawns, who were wounded in the battle. You receive a transmission from the past, but you can't remember who sent it.

You go outside. Then you realize that you have forgotten all of your things. You want to go back in, but the door through which you came out is missing, replaced by a concrete wall. You are completely naked on a windy street.

You wake up in the morning, but it's dark outside. You could be in the far North. The stars are all missing. The world must have run out of light. Everything is encrypted, and you don't know the cipher yet.

You remember being willing to share your time with others, but others did not share with you. Your supplies have run dry. The blind person is at the end of the block, waving a cane. You know the signals are meant for you. But you can't remember how you concluded this.

> Your history is more ancient with every day. Before a moment passes, it is already registered in the catalog of the past. The catalog is not yet alphabetized. A few pawns are picking on a rook in the space between the ocean and the river.

You go outside, but the outside is gone. It's like a vast empty field, but without a field. It's like you, but without you. You have brought a library of building blocks from which you will construct it all over, every day. You must create yourself and the world around you. This is your life as it is.

About the Author

Born in Russia, A. Molotkov moved to the US in 1990 and switched to writing in English in 1993. Published or accepted by *The Kenyon Review, Mad Hatters Review, 2River, Perihelion, Word Riot, Identity Theory, Pif,* and many more, Molotkov is winner of New Millennium Writings and Koeppel fiction contests, and a poetry chapbook contest for his *True Stories from the Future*. He co-edits *The Inflectionist Review* and serves on the Board of Directors of Oregon Poetry Association. Molotkov's new translation of a Chekhov story was included by Knopf in their Everyman Series. Visit him at *AMolotkov.com*.

www.ingramcontent.com/pod-product-compliance
Lightning Source LLC
Chambersburg PA
CBHW021200080526
44588CB00008B/439